Chocolate Lover's Cookbook:
60 Super #Delish Chocolate Recipes

RHONDA BELLE

ISBN-13: 978-1539812814

ISBN-10: 1539812812

DEDICATION

To Foodies Everywhere...Enjoy & Be Well!

Table of Contents

ACKNOWLEDGEMENTS

To the love of my life, Johnny.
You are Mommy's greatest inspiration.

To Mom & Dad (Sunset February 2016).
Love you always...

Why We Love Chocolate

Chocolate is truly heaven-scent! It smells great, tastes great and has the power to make us fantastic. The melt-in-your-mouth goodness that chocolate offers comes from its perfect blend of sugar, fat and cocoa compounds that are #delish and also release dopamine (the body's pleasure cocktail that we experience when we fall in love!).

Find new and fun ways to enjoy the rich creamy pleasure of nature's sweetest treasure with these great chocolate recipes. Enjoy!

Afternoon Tea Brownies

¼ cup vegetable shortening
½ cup granulated sugar replacement
½ cup pecans, toasted and ground
½ cup skim milk
½ teaspoon salt
1 cup cake flower
1 ounce baking chocolate, melted
1 teaspoon baking powder
2 tablespoons cocoa
3 eggs

Sift flower, salt, baking powder and cocoa together. Pour melted chocolate over shortening and stir until completely blended. Beat eggs until thick; gradually add sugar replacement. Add chocolate mixture and small amount of flower mixture. Beat to thoroughly blend. Add remaining flour mixture alternately with milk. Fold in the pecans. Spread into two greased 8-inch pans. Bake at 325 degrees for about 20 minutes. Remove from oven and allow to cool. Cut into bars and enjoy!

Apple Brownies

¾ cup nuts of choice
¾ teaspoon baking powder
¾ teaspoon cinnamon
¾ teaspoon baking soda
1½ cups flour
1½ cups sugar
1½ stick margarine
2 eggs
3 crisp apples, chopped

Cream margarine, sugar and eggs. Add flour, soda, baking powder and cinnamon; mix well. Stir in apples and nuts. Bake at 375 degrees for 40 minutes. Remove from oven and cool. Cut and serve warm, preferably with ice cream. #Delish!

Banana Cream Brownie Squares

¾ cup dry roasted peanuts, chopped
1 package (15 ounces) brownie mix
1 tub Cool Whip, thawed
1¼ cup milk
2 medium bananas, sliced
51/8 ounces instant vanilla pudding
About 9 fresh strawberries

Prepare brownie mix according to package directions & stir in ½ cup chopped peanuts. Pour into a greased 9-inch square pan. Bake at 350 degrees for 25 minutes. Cool completely. Layer 2 of the sliced bananas over the brownie. Whisk pudding mix & milk together until pudding just begins to thicken. Fold in 2½ cups of Cool Whip. Quickly spread pudding mixture over the sliced bananas. Refrigerate for 30 minutes. Sprinkle remaining ¼ cup peanuts over pudding mixture. *For an elegant serving presentation*: Pipe remaining Cool Whip over the squares. Grate chocolate over the dessert. Top each square with banana & strawberry slices. Enjoy!

Banana Nut Chocolate Chip Bread

¼ teaspoon baking soda
1/3 cup butter or margarine, softened
½ cup buttermilk
½ cup chocolate chips (or more if desired)
½ teaspoon salt
¾ cup white sugar
1 cup chopped pecans or walnuts
1 cup mashed banana
1 egg
2 cups all-purpose flour
2½ teaspoons baking powder

Preheat oven to 350 degrees. Cream butter and sugar. Mix in egg and banana. Stir together flour, baking powder, baking soda, salt, nuts and chocolate chips. Add this mixture to creamed mixture alternately with buttermilk. Stir until just blended. Pour batter into a greased and floured loaf pan. Bake for 65 minutes or until the bread tests done. Cool in pan for about 5 minutes, then turn out on a wire rack to cool. #Delish!

Berry Brownie Pizza

¼ cup sugar
¼ cup vegetable oil
1/3 cup cold water
1 egg
1 egg
1 package (8 ounces) favorite cream cheese, softened
1 teaspoon vanilla
2 (1 ounce each) squares baker's semi-sweet chocolate, melted
Banana slices
Brownie mix of choice
Strawberry slices

Preheat oven to 350 degrees. Bring water to a boil. Mix together brownie mix, water, oil and egg in large bowl until well blended. Pour into greased and floured 12" pizza pan. Bake for 25 minutes. Next, beat cream cheese sugar, egg and vanilla in small mixing bowl at medium speed until well blended. Pour over crust. Bake 15 minutes. Cool. Top with fruit. Drizzle with chocolate. #Delish!

Black Forest Brownies

¼ cup oil
1 cup cherry pie filling
1 cup semi-sweet chocolate chips
1 package brownie mix
2 cups low-fat vanilla ice cream
2 egg whites, whipped

Preheat oven to 350 degrees. Prepare a 9" x 13" pan with cooking spray and flour; set aside. In a mixing bowl, combine brownie mix, cherry pie filling, oil, and egg whites. Pour into prepared pan. Bake for 30 minutes. Remove from oven, sprinkle with chocolate chips. Spread when melted and serve with ice cream. Enjoy!

Blondie Bombshells

1/8 teaspoon salt
½ cup butter flavor Crisco
½ cup walnuts, chopped
½ teaspoon baking powder
1 cup brown sugar, firmly packed
1 cup flour, all purpose
1 egg
1 tablespoon milk
1 teaspoon vanilla

Heat oven to 350 degrees. Grease a baking dish pan with a little butter flavor Crisco. Set aside. Combine Butter Flavor Crisco and milk in large saucepan. Place on low heat until Crisco melts. Remove from heat. Stir in brown sugar. Add egg. Stir until well blended. Combine flour, baking powder and salt. Stir into sugar mixture. Then stir in vanilla and nuts. Spread evenly into baking pan. Bake at 350 degrees 30 minutes, or until a wooden pick inserted into center comes out clean. Cool in pan. Cut into 2x2 inch squares. #Delish!

Bourbon Chocolate Cake

1/3 cup vegetable oil
½ cup bourbon whiskey
½ cup water; cold
1 package chocolate cake mix with pudding added
3 eggs
FROSTING:
1/3 cup unsweetened cocoa powder
½ cup bourbon
½ cup powdered sugar
1 cup nuts of choice, chopped
1 pint whipping cream
1 teaspoon vanilla

Butter and flour two 9" round cake pans. Combine cake mix, eggs, bourbon whisky, cold water and vegetable oil in large bowl of mixer. Beat for 2 minutes on high speed until very light. Pour into pans. Bake at 350 degrees for 30 minutes or until tests done. Cool in pans 10 minutes. Remove. Cool completely. Split layers in half horizontally. Spread frosting over each cake layer. Sprinkle with walnuts. Stack layers. Cover sides with frosting. Chill at least 2 hours. *To make frosting*: In large mixing bowl, combine whipping cream, cocoa, powdered sugar, and vanilla. Beat until stiff then fold in the bourbon. Frost, slice and enjoy!

Cappuccino Chocolate Cheesecake

1/8 teaspoon cinnamon
1 cup sugar
1 cup unsweetened cocoa powder
1 package (8 ounces) light cream cheese
1 teaspoon cocoa powder for garnish
1 teaspoon vanilla
1¼ cup chocolate wafers, crushed
2½ cups sour cream
2 eggs
2 tablespoons coffee liqueur

Preheat oven to 350 degrees. Stir together wafer crumbs and cinnamon. Pat into the bottom of 9" spring form pan. Beat cream cheese until light and fluffy. Beat in sugar and cocoa powder. Beat in egg. Stir in 2 cups sour cream, coffee liqueur and vanilla. Pour into a prepared pan. Bake for 30 minutes or until set. Spread remaining sour cream evenly over the top. Return to oven for 1 minute so that glaze can set. Cool to room temperature, cover, then chill thoroughly. Remove from pan. Just before serving, dust top with cocoa powder. #Delish!

Caramel Chocolate Chip Cake

½ cup granulated sugar
½ cup semi-sweet chocolate chips, finely chopped
½ cup shortening
½ teaspoon baking soda
1¼ cup milk
1 small container of caramel frosting
1 cup packed brown sugar
1 teaspoon salt
1½ teaspoon vanilla extract
2 cups all-purpose flour
3 eggs
3 teaspoons baking powder

Preheat oven to 350 degrees. Grease and flour a 9" x 13" rectangular baking pan. Beat all ingredients except frosting in a large bowl on low speed for 30 seconds, scraping bowl constantly. Beat on high speed for 3 minutes, scraping bowl occasionally. Pour into prepared pan. Bake until the cake tests clean, about 40 to 45 minutes; cool completely. Frost and serve. #Delish!

Chewy Chocolate Rolls

¼ teaspoon salt
½ cup light corn syrup
¾ cup powered dry milk
1 teaspoon vanilla
2 ounces chocolate, melted
2 tablespoons butter
3 cups confectioners' sugar

Mix together butter, syrup, chocolate, vanilla, powdered milk, and salt. Gradually add confectioners' sugar; mix and knead. Roll out in ¾-inch rolls, cut into 2 ½-inch lengths. Let stand for about one hour, then wrap in plastic wrap for about 18 rolls. Enjoy!

Choco-Caramel Nut Bars

½ cup margarine, melted
1 (14 ounces) bag caramels, wrappers removed
1 (5 ounces) can evaporated milk
1 box German chocolate cake mix with pudding
1½ cup walnuts, chopped
6 ounces semi-sweet chocolate chips

Melt caramels with 1/3 cup milk in the microwave. Stir until smooth. Combine remaining milk, mix and margarine. Mix well. Press half of cake mixture into the bottom of a greased 9" x 13" baking pan. Bake 350 degrees for 6 minutes. Sprinkle with 1 cup walnuts, chocolate pieces over the crust; top with caramel mixture spreading to the edges of the pan. Top with teaspoonfuls of remaining cake mixture. Sprinkle with walnuts (press them lightly into the top). Bake for 350 degrees for 20 minutes. Cool slightly; cut into bars. #Delish!

Chocolate Almond Pound Cake

½ cup almonds, finely chopped
½ teaspoon baking powder
1 cup corn meal
1 cup milk
1 teaspoon salt
1½ cup sugar
1½ teaspoon almond extract
2 cups flour
4 eggs
4 ounces bitter chocolate, melted
4 ounces butter, melted

Preheat oven to 350 degrees. Generously grease a 12 cup Bundt pan. Coat sides with almonds. In a large bowl, beat sugar and butter until light and fluffy. Add eggs, one at a time, mixing well after each egg. Stir in chocolate and almond extract. Combine flour, corn meal, salt and baking powder. Add alternately, with milk, to the chocolate mixture, mixing at low speed until well blended. Spoon into baking pan. Bake 50-60 minutes. Cool 10 minutes. Remove from pan and allow to cool completely before serving. #Delish!

Chocolate Angel Food Cake

¼ cup cocoa
½ teaspoon salt
1 cup all-purpose flour
10 egg whites
1½ cups sugar
1½ teaspoons cream of tartar
1½ teaspoons vanilla

Preheat oven to 325 degrees. In medium bowl, sift flour. Sift flour again twice with cocoa and ½ cup sugar. Set aside. In large bowl, beat egg whites, cream of tartar, and salt until soft peaks form. Gradually add remaining sugar, 2 tablespoons at a time until stiff peaks form. Fold in flour mixture and vanilla. Pour into ungreased tube pan. Bake for 1 hour. Invert pan for about 1 hour or until the cake is cool. Remove, slice and enjoy!

Chocolate Beer Cake

BATTER:
¼ teaspoon salt
½ teaspoon baking soda
¾ cup beer
¾ cup sugar
1 egg, slightly beaten
1 tablespoon unsweetened cocoa
1½ cup all-purpose flour
1½ teaspoon baking powder
1/3 cup oil
SYRUP:
1/3 cup granulated sugar
1/3 cup packed brown sugar
¾ cup beer
1 tablespoon unsweetened cocoa

For batter: Mix dry ingredients and make a well in center; add beer, oil and egg. Beat smooth. *For syrup:* Make a paste of cocoa, beer and sugars. Add to a small saucepan and heat to boiling. Pour batter into a greased 8-inch square baking dish. Drizzle syrup over top. Bake at 350 degrees for 40 minutes. Cool for 5 minutes. Loosen sides of cake from pan; invert onto platter. #Delish!

Chocolate Biscotti

½ cup butter
½ teaspoon baking powder
½ teaspoon vanilla extract
1¼ cups sugar
1 cup hazelnuts or walnuts; chop
1 egg white; lightly beaten
3 cup all-purpose flour
3 large eggs
4 ounces unsweetened chocolate

Melt chocolate and butter in a heavy saucepan over low heat. Beat eggs at medium speed with an electric mixer until frothy; gradually add sugar, beating until thick and pale (about 5 minutes). Add chocolate mixture, stirring until blended. Combine flour and baking powder; stir into chocolate mixture. Stir in nuts. Flour hands, and form dough into a 13" log. Place on a lightly greased baking sheet. Brush with egg white. Bake at 350 degrees for 45 minutes; cool on a wire rack. Cut log with a serrated knife crosswise into 24 (½-inch) slices, and place on an ungreased cookie sheet. Bake at 350 degrees for 10 minutes on each side. Move to wire racks to cool and then serve. #Delish!

Chocolate Brittle

1 lb. whole walnuts
1 lb. almonds
1 lb. semi-sweet chocolate
1 lb. sugar
1 lb. walnuts, finely chopped

In a saucepan cook butter and sugar, boiling 5 minutes. Stir in almonds and cook 10-20 minutes or until nuts begin to pop and turn brown. Pour into a shallow pan and let cool. Melt chocolate and pour over mixture in pan. Sprinkle with finely chopped walnuts. After mixture hardens, turn over and sprinkle bottom with walnuts. Break candy into pieces. Share & enjoy!

Chocolate Caramel Shortbread

¼ teaspoon salt
½ cup sifted icing sugar
1 ¼ cup all-purpose flour
1 can sweetened condensed milk
1 teaspoon vanilla
1½ cups butter, softened and divided
3 squares semi-sweet chocolate, melted
3 tablespoons corn syrup

Preheat oven to 350 degrees. In large mixer bowl, beat 1 cup butter, sugar and salt until fluffy. Add flour; mix well. With floured finger, press evenly into greased 9 inch square pan. Bake 30-35 minutes or until lightly browned. Cool slightly. While cooling, microwave melt the remaining ½ cup butter (about 1 minute). Stir in sweetened condensed milk and corn syrup. Microwave on high for 6-8 minutes, stirring after each minute, or until mixture turns a light caramel color. Stir in vanilla. Spread over warm shortbread. Drizzle with chocolate. Chill until firm. Cut into bars and enjoy!

Chocolate Carrot Cake

½ cup canola oil
½ cup unsweetened cocoa powder
½ teaspoon salt
¾ cup granulated sugar
1 cup boiling water
1 teaspoon cinnamon
1½ cups finely grated carrots
1½ cups whole-wheat flour
1½ teaspoons baking powder

Pre-heat oven to 350 degrees. In a large bowl, combine carrots, sugar & oil. Pour water over the mixture. In a separate bowl, combine the rest of the ingredients. Add to the carrot mixture & mix well. Pour into a non-stick or lightly oiled 8" square pan. Bake for 35 minutes. Remove, cool, slice and enjoy!

Chocolate Chip Cookie Bars

½ cup chopped nuts or shelled
½ cup margarine or butter, softened
½ cup shortening
½ cup white sugar
½ teaspoon salt
¾ cup firmly packed brown sugar
1¾ cups all-purpose flour
1 cup semi-sweet chocolate chips
1 egg
1 teaspoon baking soda
1½ teaspoons vanilla
Sunflower seeds (optional)

Heat oven to 375 degrees. In large bowl, combine sugars, margarine and shortening; beat until light and fluffy. Add vanilla and egg; blend well. Stir in flour, baking soda, and salt; mix well. Stir in chocolate chips and nuts. Spread in ungreased 9" x 13" baking pan. Bake for 15 to 25 minutes or until light golden brown. Cool completely. Cut into bars. #Delish!

Chocolate Chip Lollipops

1 egg
1 package Duncan Hines chocolate chip cookie mix
2 teaspoon water
24 flat ice cream sticks
Assorted decors such as rainbow sprinkles, untoasted coconut, etc.

Preheat oven to 375 degrees F. Combine cookie mix, egg and water in large bowl. Stir until thoroughly blended. Shape dough into 24 (1") balls. Place balls 3" apart on ungreased baking sheets. Push ice cream stick into center of each ball. Flatten each ball with hand to form round lollipop. Decorate by pressing decors onto dough. Bake at 375 degrees for 8-9 minutes or until light golden brown. Cool 1 minute on baking sheets. Remove to cooling racks. Cool completely. Enjoy!

Chocolate Coconut Candies

1 cup cold or warm mashed potatoes
1 lb. flaked coconut
1 lb. powdered sugar
1 teaspoon almond extract
1 (12 ounces) bag chocolate chips
2 tablespoons shortening

Mix potatoes, powdered sugar, and almond extract in large bowl. Stir in coconut. Drop by rounded teaspoonfuls onto waxed paper; shape into balls. If mixture is too soft, refrigerate until able to handle. Heat chocolate chips and shortening over low heat until melted. Dip 1 ball at a time until coated; place on waxed paper. Chill balls until firm. #Delish!

Chocolate Cranberry Cake

1/3 cup cake flour
½ lb. butter, softened to room temp
2/3 cup sugar
1-1/3 cups fresh cranberries, chopped
1 teaspoon vanilla
3 tablespoons cranberry liqueur
3 tablespoons sugar
4 eggs, separated
8 ounces semi-sweet chocolate, melted

Preheat oven to 350 degrees. Line bottom of a 9-inch spring form pan with parchment. Whip butter with electric beater until light and fluffy. Add sugar and beat for up to 3 minutes. Mix in vanilla, liqueur and chocolate. Add yolks one at a time. Mix in flour and cranberries. Whip egg whites in clean bowl until soft peaks form. Add 3 tablespoons sugar and continue whipping until stiff. Fold 1/3 of whites into batter. Then fold remaining whites into mixture. Pour into prepared pan and bake for 25 minutes. Let cool for 5 minutes, then cover with foil and cool completely. #Delish!

Chocolate Holiday Pretzels

1 package long pretzel rods
1 package almond bark mixed
1 cup semi-sweet chocolate chips
Decorations, such as colorful candy sprinkles, holiday M&Ms or crushed candy canes

Place the candy coating in a dry microwave-safe bowl. Microwave the bark/chocolate for 1 minute, then stir and microwave an additional minute, until it is completely melted and smooth. Dip a pretzel rod in and with a spoon, cover about ¾ of the pretzel with almond bark. Let the excess drip back into the bowl. Sprinkle the pretzel with either colored sprinkles, crushed peppermints, or M&Ms. Place the decorated pretzel on a piece of waxed paper or aluminum foil, and let it dry completely, about 1 hour. Gently pull the pretzels from the paper when ready and enjoy!

Chocolate Marshmallow Bars

½ cup butter
½ cup flour
1 cup chopped pecans
1 cup sugar
1 teaspoon vanilla
16 large marshmallows
2 eggs
2 ounces unsweetened chocolate

Preheat oven to 350 degrees. Grease a large baking pan. Melt chocolate and butter in small saucepan. Set aside. Cream sugar and eggs until light and fluffy. Add flour. Beat. Add melted chocolate and butter. Beat well. Mix in vanilla and pecans. Pour into prepared pan. Bake 18 minutes. Remove from oven and cover with marshmallows. Return to oven and bake until marshmallows are lightly browned. Cool slightly and cut into bars. #Delish!

Chocolate Raisin Bars

¼ cup vanilla sugar
1/3 cup raisins, chopped
¾ cup butter
1¾ cup all-purpose flour
1 pinch salt
8 ounces semi-sweet chocolate pieces
8 teaspoons potato flour

Preheat oven to 350 degrees. Sift all-purpose flour, salt, potato flour and vanilla sugar into a medium-size bowl. Cut in butter until mixture forms coarse crumbs; mix in raisins. Mix together to form a soft dough. Roll out dough on a floured surface to a rectangle slightly smaller than a large baking pan. Place rolled-out dough in pan; press to fit. Smooth top; prick well. Bake about 25 minutes or until very lightly browned. Cool a few minutes. Using a sharp knife, mark through surface of mixture with lines to use as a guide for cutting. Let cool in pan. Cut mixture in 20 squares; remove from pan. Next, place chocolate in a small bowl over a pan of gently simmering water; stir until melted and smooth. Line a baking sheet with foil. Dip bars in chocolate, coating evenly; lift out with a fork and tap gently on side of bowl to remove excess chocolate. Place on foil. Place baking sheet in a cool place until chocolate sets. If desired, pipe remaining chocolate over bars for decoration. #Delish!

Chocolate Truffle Loaf with Raspberry Sauce

¼ cup powdered sugar
½ cup butter
½ cup light Karo syrup
1 teaspoon vanilla
16 ounces baker's semi-sweet chocolate
2 cups heavy cream
3 egg yolks; slightly beaten
SAUCE:
1/3 cup lite Karo corn syrup
10 ounces fresh raspberries, pureed and strained
Fresh raspberries for garnish

Line a loaf pan with plastic wrap. Mix a ½ cup heavy cream with the egg yolks. In a medium saucepan, melt chocolate, corn syrup and butter over medium heat. Add the egg mixture and cook 3 minutes, stirring constantly. Cool to room temperature. Next, beat the remaining heavy cream, sugar, and vanilla to soft peak stage. Fold into the chocolate mixture and pour into the lined pan. Refrigerate overnight. The next day, stir the corn syrup into the raspberry puree. Remove chocolate loaf from pan. Serve sliced, topped with puree, a dollop of whipped cream, and a few fresh raspberries. #Delish!

Chocolate Zucchini Bread

1 cup nuts, ground
1 cup oil
1 teaspoon baking soda
1 teaspoon cinnamon
1 teaspoon salt
1 teaspoon vanilla
1 ½ teaspoon baking powder
2 cups grated zucchini
2 cups white sugar
2 squares unsweetened chocolate, melted
3 cups flour
3 eggs

Mix eggs, sugar and oil until well blended. Stir in melted chocolate and add vanilla; stir in zucchini. Add dry ingredients slowly and mix well. Pour into 2 greased loaf pans. Bake at 350 degrees for 50 minutes or until they test done. Cool and turn out on cake rack to finish cooling. Enjoy!

Chocolatey Party Poppers

½ cup Land O'Lakes butter
1 cup all-purpose flour
1 cup salted peanuts
1 teaspoon vanilla extract
10 ½ ounce marshmallows, miniature
2 ounces semi-sweet chocolate
6 cups popcorn

Combine butter, marshmallows and chocolate in a small saucepan. Cook over low heat, stirring constantly, until melted and well blended. Remove from heat. Gradually add flour and salt, mixing well. Stir in vanilla and peanuts. Pour over popcorn, mixing well. Press into a well-greased 9" x13" pan. Bake at 350 degrees for 10 to 12 minutes. Cool; cut into bars. Dust with confectioners' sugar and dig in. #Delish!

Choco-Pecan Cheesecake Bars

CRUST:
½ cup butter or margarine, softened
½ cup pecans, chopped
1 egg
1 package chocolate cake mix
FILLING:
1 egg
1 teaspoon vanilla
1 (14 ounces) sweetened condensed milk
8 ounces cream cheese, softened

Heat oven to 350. Grease 9" x 13" pan. In large bowl, combine cake mix, margarine and egg; mix at low speed until combined. Stir in pecans. Reserve 1 cup for topping; set aside. Press remaining mixture evenly in bottom of greased pan. Beat cream cheese in medium bowl until fluffy. Add remaining filling ingredients and beat at medium speed until smooth. Pour over crust; sprinkle with reserved topping. Bake at 350 degrees for 35 to 40 minutes. Cool completely. Cut into bars. #Delish!

Cinnamon Chocolate Fondue

¼ cup flour
¼ cup Kahlua
¼ cup margarine
½ teaspoon cinnamon
2 cups light corn syrup
8 ounces bittersweet chocolate

Melt margarine and chocolate. Whisk in flour until blended; cook 1 minute, stirring. Remove from heat, blend in cinnamon. Pour into fondue dish with its own heat source. Suggested dippers are bananas, strawberries, oranges, and pound food chunks.

Cocoa Chiffon Cake

½ cup cocoa
½ cup oil
½ tablespoon salt
½ teaspoon almond extract
½ teaspoon cream of tartar
¾ cup boiling water
1 cup egg whites, about 7-8, divided
1 teaspoon vanilla
1½ cups flour, sifted
1½ tablespoons baking powder
1¾ cups sugar, divided

Blend cocoa and water and allow to cool down to room temperature. Mix flour, baking powder and salt. Beat ½ of the egg yolks with half of the sugar. Next, in another bowl, beat whites with cream of tartar, gradually adding the rest of the sugar till stiff peaks form. Fold in this into the first yolk mixture and all remaining dry ingredients. Spoon into ungreased tube pan. Bake about 65 min. at 325 degrees. Invert to cool. Slice, serve, enjoy!

Dark Chocolate Banana Granola

1/8 teaspoon fine sea salt
½ tablespoon spirulina
1 cup almonds
1 cup shredded, unsweetened coconut
1 large banana
1 tablespoon cacao powder
1 tablespoon vanilla
1 teaspoon flax seeds
3 cups oats
3 tablespoons avocado oil, olive oil or melted coconut oil
3 tablespoons honey
5 ounces dark chocolate, roughly chopped
Nonstick cooking spray

Preheat oven to 350 degrees. Place peeled banana, honey, oil, spirulina, vanilla and salt together in a large bowl. Mash the banana with the other ingredients until well combined. In a medium bowl, mix together oats, almonds, and coconut. Add to the wet ingredients and stir to combine. Spread evenly on a sprayed baking sheet. Place in the oven and bake 15 minutes, stirring halfway through baking time. Bake another 15 minutes then remove from oven. Let cool and then add the dark chocolate. Combine and store in an airtight container at room temperature for up to a week. Enjoy!

Dark Desires Raspberry Smoothie
1/3 cup dark chocolate, chopped (or semi-sweet chocolate chips)
½ cup almond milk
½ cup raspberries (fresh or frozen)
3 tablespoons unsweetened or organic shredded coconut
2 tablespoons honey
6 ice cubes
2 tablespoons flax, chia, or hemp seeds or a combination (optional)
1 container (6-7ounces) Greek yogurt (plain, vanilla, or coconut)
Blend all ingredients until smooth and creamy. Enjoy!

Death by Chocolate
½ cup vegetable oil
½ cup water
½ teaspoon instant coffee
1 box chocolate or devil's food cake mix
1 small box of instant chocolate pudding
12 ounce bag mini chocolate chips
4 eggs
8 ounces sour cream
Beat eggs. Mix in water, oil and sour cream. Add dry ingredients and beat until smooth. Stir in chocolate chops last. Pour into a greased Bundt pan, and bake 1 hour at 350 degrees. Remove from oven and cool for a few minutes before serving. #Delish!

Easy Chocolate Ice Box Cake
½ pint whipping cream
4 egg whites, beaten stiffly
4 egg yolks, beaten
4 large Hershey bars, melted
Vanilla wafers
Pour beaten egg yolks over melted chocolate, add stiffly beaten egg whites and ½ pint whipping cream (beaten). Alternate this mixture in layers with vanilla wafers. Chill before serving. #Delish!

Easy Homemade Chocolate Candy Bar

1 envelope hot cocoa mix
1 teaspoon chopped nuts
1 teaspoon peanut butter
2 tablespoons cold water
2 tablespoons golden raisins

In small bowl stir cocoa mix with water. *Save envelope that mix came in.* Stir in raisins, peanut butter and nuts. Spoon mixture back into cocoa envelope. Fold over top and let stand against wall in bottom of freezer for about 4 hours. When frozen peel off envelope and eat. #Delish!

Fat Free Chocolate Cake

¼ cup Argo corn starch
½ cup Karo light corn syrup
½ cup unsweetened cocoa
½ teaspoon baking soda
½ teaspoon salt
1 cup water
1 teaspoon baking powder
1¼ cups sugar
1-1/3 cups flour
3 egg whites

Preheat oven to 350 degrees. Spray a square baking pan with cooking spray. In a large bowl combine flour, cocoa, cornstarch, baking powder and salt. In a medium bowl with wire whisk or fork, stir together sugar and water for 1 minute. Next, add egg whites and corn syrup; stir until blended. Gradually stir into dry ingredients until smooth. Pour into pan. Bake 35 minutes or until an inserted toothpick tests clean. Cool. If desired, sprinkle with confectioner's sugar. #Delish!

Fudge Balls

2/3 cup evaporated milk
1 cup chopped nuts
12 ounces semi-sweet chocolate bits
2½ cups powdered sugar
7 ounces shredded coconut

Mix chocolate bits and milk. Microwave until melted, about 3 minutes. Stir in sugar, and nuts. Chill for ½ hour. Roll into balls. Color coconut and roll balls in the coconut. #Delish!

German Chocolate Chip Bread

½ cup of water
1 cup of chopped nuts
10 eggs
1½ cups of oil
12 ounces of chocolate chips
12 ounces sour cream
2 boxes of German Chocolate cake mix
2 small boxes of chocolate instant pudding

Mix together all ingredients. Pour into three greased loaf pans. Bake at 325 degrees for one hour or until done when tested with a wooden pick. Remove from oven and let cool a bit. Serve warm. #Delish!

Gooey Caramel Chocolate Bars

2/3 cup evaporated milk, divided
¾ cup margarine, melted
1 cup chocolate chips
1 cup walnuts, chopped
1 German chocolate cake mix
1 (14 ounces) bag caramels

Melt caramels and 1/3 cup evaporated milk over hot water or in microwave, stirring every thirty seconds. Keep warm. Mix the cake mix, margarine and 1/3 cup evaporated milk and beat well. Spread ½ the batter in a greased 9" x13" inch pan. Bake for 6 minutes at 350 degrees. Cool for at least 2 minutes. Next, spread caramel mixture over baked layer and sprinkle with chocolate chips. Stir ½ cup nuts into remaining ½ of batter and drop by ½ teaspoonfuls over top. Sprinkle with remaining ½ cup nuts. Return to oven and bake for 18 minutes at 350 degrees. Cool in pan and cut into 1½ inch squares. #Delish!

Homemade Chocolate Cake

½ teaspoon of salt
¾ cup of cocoa
1 cup of boiling water
1 cup of milk
1 teaspoon of baking powder
1 teaspoon of baking soda
1 teaspoon of butter
1 teaspoon of vanilla
2 cups of plain flour
2 cups of sugar
2 eggs

Beat the sugar, eggs and butter together until creamy. Add the cocoa to 1 cup of boiling water and mix well. Add cocoa mixture to sugar mixture. Sift flour, soda, baking powder and salt together. Add to the sugar mixture alternating with the milk and vanilla, starting and ending with the flour mixture. Pour into well-greased and floured pans and bake at 350 degrees for 25 to 30 minutes.
FROSTING:
½ cup of milk

1 ½ cup of sugar
1 teaspoon of vanilla
2 (1 ounce) squares of chocolate
2 tablespoons of butter

Melt the chocolate in a pan and remove from heat. Mix in the sugar and milk and bring to a full boil. Cook the chocolate mixture until it reaches the "soft ball stage" (a small amount dropped into a glass of cold water forms a soft ball). Remove the chocolate mixture from the heat and stir in the vanilla and butter. Spread on the cooled cake. #Delish!

Homemade Dark Chocolate Fudge

1 can (14 ounces) sweetened condensed milk
1 cup chopped walnuts
1½ teaspoons vanilla
3 cups semi-sweet chocolate chips
Dash of salt

In heavy saucepan over low heat, melt chips with sweetened condensed milk and salt. Remove from heat; stir in walnuts and vanilla. Spread evenly into an aluminum foil lined 8 or 9 inch square pan. Chill for 2 hours or until firm. Turn fudge onto cutting board; peel off foil and cut into squares. Store loosely covered at room temperature. #Delish!

Hot Fudge Sundae Cake

¼ teaspoon salt
½ cup milk
¾ cup sugar
1¾ cups hot tap water
1 cup brown sugar
1 cup chopped nuts
1 cup flour
1 teaspoon vanilla
2 tablespoons cocoa
2 tablespoons salad oil
2 teaspoons baking powder
Ice cream

Heat oven to 350 degrees. In an ungreased square pan stir together flour, sugar, cocoa, baking powder, and salt. Mix in milk, oil and vanilla with fork until smooth. Stir in nuts. Spread evenly in pan. Sprinkle with brown sugar and ¼ cup cocoa. Pour hot water over batter. Bake for 40 minutes. Let stand for 15 minutes. Spoon into dessert dishes or cut into squares. Invert each square onto dessert plate. Top with ice cream and spoon sauce over each square. #Delish!

Maple Choco-Bars

½ teaspoon salt
2/3 cup sugar
¾ cup margarine or butter, unmelted
1 cup semi-sweet chocolate chips
1½ cups flour, unsifted
1½ teaspoons maple flavoring
14 ounces sweetened condensed milk
2 cups nuts of choice, chopped
2 eggs

Preheat oven to 350 degrees. In a large bowl, combine flour, sugar and salt; cut in margarine until crumbly. Stir in 1 beaten egg. Press evenly in a 9x13" pan. Bake for 25 minutes. Meanwhile, in medium bowl, beat sweetened condensed milk, remaining egg and flavoring; stir in nuts. Sprinkle chocolate chips evenly over the prepared crust. Top with the nut mixture. Bake for 25 minutes more or until lightly brown. Cool. Cut into bars. #Delish!

Mini Chocolate Chip Cheesecake Ball

½ cup butter, softened
½ teaspoon vanilla extract
¾ cup confectioners' sugar
¾ cup finely chopped pecans
¾ cup mini semi-sweet chocolate chips
1 (8 ounces) package cream cheese, softened
2 tablespoons brown sugar

In a medium bowl, beat together cream cheese and butter until smooth. Mix in confectioners' sugar, brown sugar and vanilla. Stir in chocolate chips. Cover, and chill in the refrigerator for 2 hours. Shape chilled cream cheese mixture into a ball. Wrap with plastic, and chill in the refrigerator for 1 hour or overnight. Roll the cheese ball in finely chopped pecans before serving. Serve with chocolate graham crackers. #Delish!

Mint Chocolate Dessert Balls

½ cup Crème de Menthe
1 teaspoon cinnamon, ground
2 cups pecans; finely chopped
24 ounces cream cheese, softened
9 ounces chocolate chips, melted
Chocolate cookie wafers

In large bowl, mix together ingredients except pecans until smooth. Cover and chill 1 hour. Take small, palm-sized amounts of mixture and form into balls. Roll balls in pecans and rest them on a cookie sheet lined with parchment papers to set. Serve with chocolate cookie wafers. #Delish!

Mud Bars

1/3 cup cocoa
½ cup evaporated milk
½ cup margarine
1 cup chopped walnuts
1 cup margarine
1½ cup all-purpose flour
2 cups sugar
3 cups miniature marshmallows
4 cups icing sugar
4 eggs

Cream margarine and sugar until light and fluffy. Add eggs, one at a time, beating well after each addition. Sift cocoa and flour together, beat in gradually. Stir in walnuts. Spoon batter into a greased 9" x 13" inch pan. Bake at 350 degrees for 30 - 35 minutes. Immediately sprinkle top of cake with marshmallows. Return to oven for 3 - 5 minutes until marshmallows are slightly puffed. Cool for half-hour. *For icing*: Cream margarine and combine icing sugar and cocoa (beat in alternately with milk). Beat until icing is light and fluffy. Spread over marshmallow layer. Chill to serve; cut into bars. #Delish!

Nana's Chocolate Cake

¼ cup instant dry milk
¼ cup sugar
1/3 cup cocoa
1/3 cup sugar
½ cup liquid egg substitute
¾ cup margarine, at room temperature
1 cup water
2 cups cake flour
2 teaspoons baking powder
2 teaspoons vanilla

Cream together margarine and sugar at medium speed until light and fluffy. Add egg substitute, sweetener, and vanilla to creamed mixture and beat at medium speed for ½ minute. Stir together flour, baking powder, dry milk, and cocoa to blend. Add 1 cup water to creamed mixture along with flour mixture and mix at medium speed only until smooth. Spread evenly in a square pan that has been greased with margarine. Bake at 350 degrees for 30-35 minutes or until a cake tests clean. Cool to room temperature before cutting. #Delish!

Oatmeal Chocolate Chip Bars

¾ cup nuts, chopped
1 cup flour
1 cup shortening
1 teaspoon baking soda
1 teaspoon salt
1½ cups brown sugar, packed
12 ounces semi-sweet chocolate chips
2 tablespoons molasses
2 teaspoons vanilla
2 whole eggs
3 cups rolled oats

Preheat oven to 350 degrees. Grease 9" x 13" baking pan. In large bowl, beat brown sugar and shortening until light and fluffy. Add molasses, vanilla, and eggs; blend well. Lightly spoon flour into measuring cup; level off. Stir in oats, flour, baking soda and salt; blend well. Stir in nuts and chocolate chips. Spread in prepared pan. Bake at 350 degrees for 20 to 25 minutes or until light golden brown and center is set. Cool slightly; cut into bars. Serve and enjoy!

Perfect Peppermint Patties

¼ cup evaporated milk
½ teaspoon vanilla extract
1 lb. confectioners' sugar
2 cups (12 ounces) semi-sweet chocolate chips
2 tablespoons shortening
2 -3 teaspoons peppermint extract
3 teaspoons butter or margarine, softened

In a bowl, combine sugar, butter, mint extract and vanilla. Add milk and mix well. Roll into 1" balls and place on a waxed paper-lined cookie sheet. Chill in the fridge for 20 minutes. Flatten to ¼" (try using the bottom of a juice glass) Chill for 30 minutes. In a double boiler or microwave-safe bowl, melt chocolate chips and shortening. Dip patties and place on waxed paper to harden. Easy and #delish!

Pretty Peach Chocolate Cake

¼ cup cocoa powder
¼ cup oil
½ teaspoon salt
1 cup sugar
1 cup water
1 teaspoon baking soda
1 teaspoon vanilla extract
1 teaspoon vinegar
1½ cups flour
2 cups peach slices

Combine flour, sugar, cocoa, baking soda and salt in a large bowl. Add water, oil, vinegar and vanilla extract. Whisk just until batter is smooth and ingredients are well blended. Pour into round cake pans that have been sprayed with nonstick vegetable spray. Bake at 350 degrees for 20 to 25 minutes or until cake tests clean. Cool 10 minutes, then remove from pan. Cool completely on a wire rack. Just before serving, place 1 layer on serving plate and arrange 1 cup peach slices on top. Top with second cake layer and remaining peaches.

Pudding Brownies

¼ teaspoon baking powder
1/3 cup butter
½ cup nuts; chopped
½ cup unsifted flour
2/3 cup sugar
1 package (4 ounces) chocolate pudding
1 teaspoon vanilla
2 eggs

Combine flour, pudding mix and baking powder. Mix well. Melt butter in sauce pan. Remove from heat. Beat eggs in one at a time. Blend in vanilla and pudding mixture. Spread in 8" square pan and bake at 350 degrees for 35 minutes. Do not overbake. Cool in pan. Cut into bars. #Delish!

Quickie Chocolate Pudding

1/8 teaspoon salt
½ cup granulated sugar
2/3 cup unsweetened cocoa powder
1 teaspoon vanilla extract
2 egg whites
2 tablespoons cornstarch
2¼ cup milk, nonfat (divided)

In a small bowl, lightly beat egg whites and set aside. In a large bowl, combine cocoa and cornstarch. Whisk ¾ cup of milk into cocoa mixture until completely smooth. In a large heavy saucepan, combine remaining milk, sugar, and salt. Mix well. Bring to a boil over high heat, whisking constantly. Remove pan from heat. Whisk cocoa mixture into hot milk mixture. Bring to a boil over medium-high heat. Boil for 2 minutes, whisking constantly. Remove pan from heat. Gradually whisk 1 cup hot cocoa mixture into egg whites. Pour mixture back into pan. Cook over medium-low heat for 2 minutes, whisking constantly. DO NOT BOIL! Remove from heat and add vanilla; blend well. Pour into serving dishes. Cool to room temperature and then cover and chill for 1 hour. Garnish with fresh strawberries, mint leaves and a dusting of cocoa powder. #Delish!

Rich Chocolate Brownies

¼ teaspoon salt
½ cup broken walnut meats
½ cup semi-sweet chocolate chips
½ cups margarine or butter
¾ cups flour
1 cup sugar
1 ripe banana, well mashed
1 teaspoon vanilla
1½ squares unsweetened chocolate
2 eggs

No baking powder or soda. This makes them extra dense and moist. Preheat oven to 350 degrees (325 for glass baking dishes). Combine flour and salt in a small bowl. Set aside. Melt margarine or butter and unsweetened chocolate in a small pan on low heat. Cool to room temperature. In a large bowl, beat eggs, sugar and vanilla. Add mashed banana. Stir in chocolate mixture. Gradually sift and stir in flour mixture. Add chocolate chips and walnuts. Pour into a greased 8"x 8"baking pan. Bake for 30 to 35 minutes. Remove, cool, and enjoy!

Skinny Brownies

¼ cup nuts, optional
½ cup flour
½ cup unsweetened cocoa powder
1 cup sugar
1 teaspoon salt
1 teaspoon vanilla
3 egg whites
4 ounce jar prune baby food

Preheat oven to 350 degrees. Spray an 8" square baking pan with cooking spray. Combine all ingredients. Add nuts if desired. Bake about 30 minutes or until springy to touch. Cool before cutting. #Delish!

Strawberry Chocolate for Two

½ cup part-skim ricotta cheese
½ ounce chocolate chips
1 cup strawberries, sliced
1 tablespoon strawberry liqueur
1½ teaspoons each granulated sugar and whipping cream

In small mixing bowl combine strawberries and liqueur; set aside. Using a fork, in separate small mixing bowl, blend cheese, sugar, and cream; fold in chips. Spoon into two long-stem dessert glasses - half of the cheese mixture, then top each with half of the strawberry mixture. Serve immediately or cover and refrigerate until chilled. #Delish!

Sweet Vienna Chocolate

¼ teaspoon salt
1 (10 ounces) raspberry jelly, seedless
1 cup semi-sweet chocolate chips
1½ cup sugar
2½ cups flour
2 egg yolks
2 sticks butter
4 egg whites

Preheat oven to 350 degrees. Cream butter with egg yolks and ½ cup sugar. Add flour and knead with fingers. Pat batter out with fingers on greased cookie sheet to about 3/8" thickness. Bake for 15 to 20 minutes until lightly browned. Remove from oven. Spread with jelly and top with chocolate chips. Beat egg whites and salt until stiff peaks form. Fold in remaining cup of sugar. Gently spread on top. Bake for additional 24 minutes. Cool and cut into bars. #Delish!

Triple Chocolate Candy Cane Kisses

½ cup crushed candy canes
4 (3 ounces each) chocolate bars - 2 semi-sweet, 1 milk & 1 white chocolate

Melt the 3 kinds of chocolate in 3 separate bowls. Stir half of the crushed candy into the semi-sweet chocolate. Reserve a bit for sprinkling; stir the remainder into the milk and white chocolates. Drop teaspoons of the semi-sweet onto a parchment-lined tray. #Delish!

World Class Chocolate Cupcakes

¼ cup oil
¼ teaspoon cinnamon
¼ teaspoon salt
1/3 cup unsweetened cocoa powder
2/3 cup milk
¾ cup sugar
1 cup all-purpose flour
1 egg
1 teaspoon baking soda
1 teaspoon vanilla
2 tablespoons lemon juice

Beat oil and sugar with egg with an electric mixer until smooth. Beat in vanilla, salt, and baking soda until well blended. Put milk and lemon juice together in cup until curdled and pour into batter, beating to blend well. Beat in cocoa powder and finally the flour, beating 3 minutes after last addition, scraping down sides and bottom of bowl often. Divide batter equally between 12 paper-lined cupcake wells. Bake at a 350 degree for 25 minutes or until cakes test clean. Cool in pan on rack 20 minutes. Remove to platter to continue cooling. Frost as desired. #Delish!

Thank you for your purchase!
May you enjoy and be well!

ABOUT THE AUTHOR

I am a Tennessee native and a connoisseur of good eats. My culinary delights are inspired by my Southern roots.

I am from cornbread and cabbage, fried chicken and Kool-Aid soaked lemon slices.

I am from hen houses, persimmon trees and juicy, red tomatoes on the vine.

I am from sunflowers growing wild in summer and homemade ice cream in the winter.

I am from family reunions, blue collar men, happy housewives, and Sunday dinners.

I am from spiritual folks who didn't always get it right, but believed in the power of prayer – and taught it to their kids.

I am from the hottest of hot summers and kids running barefoot and free through thirsty Tennessee grass.

I am from a grandmother who sang gospel that was magic...song drenched air would tumble from her lungs, leap into your spirit and make you feel fantastic things.

I am from hard, heartfelt lessons about living and kitchens full of the perfume of love.

♥♥♥ *This book is from my heart to yours.* ♥♥♥

For info, freebies & new book notices, follow @SoDelishDish on social media!
Scan with your smartphone!

FIND MORE BOOKS ONLINE

Printed in Great Britain
by Amazon